The IDIOTS HANDBOOK OF

Helen Seymore

IDEAS UNLIMITED (PUBLISHING)

© 1992 Ideas Unlimited Publishing

PO Box 125, Portsmouth PO1 4PP

ISBN 1 871964 08 3

Illustrations By Billy Sastead

Limericks by Liz Garrard & Ian Churchill

Printed in Britain by Collins, Glasgow

TO THE ONE I LOVE
WHOSE EGO, I KNOW, IS STRONG ENOUGH TO WITHSTAND
THE SEVEREST CRITICISM,

AND

WHO IS OPEN TO IDEAS

EVEN THOSE SUGGESTED ON
PAGE..50..OF THIS BOOK.

ALL MY LOVE

...............*Fat So!*...............
X

Acknowledgements

We wish to convey our gratitude to Helen Seymore for her insight into the understanding of the opposite sex.

Liz Garrad for her excellent limericks, which shed light on those very sticky situations.

Billy Sarstead for the cartoons without which the book would have been meaningless to many.

Ian Churchill for the limericks on pages 53, 61, 85, and his work for the design of the cover.

But most of all to you the readers whose support is needed to allow the publication of books such as this, where very serious subjects are discussed and communicated through humour, and thus creating a better understanding for a happier life.

An Apology

We would like to convey our sincere apologies (say sorry) to any idiot who may have been offended by (didn't like) any sections contained in this book.

Also, we acknowledge the fact that sections of this book may appear to the naked eye to be a little sexist, and that men are not in fact as bad as parts of the book imply....They are worse!!!!

Only fools, complete idiots and absolute morans would turn to page...37.....

Introduction

The subject of love and Sex has always been amongst the most documented and publicised subjects. Apart from the extensive coverage in books, magazines and newspapers, it is also unavoidable on television and the cinema.

The reason for this is very simple. It is a well known fact that the human brain (particularly that of the male species) actually transmitts one brain wave/thought about sex every ten seconds. Although they only last eight seconds at a time, it is still a subject very much on people's minds.

This book is not unlike the many books available on the subject, with the difference that it is aimed at the majority of the population who go through the maze of the complex issues connected with love and sex without clear understanding of the component parts.

An idiot in this context is a person who lacks understanding on a subject without the effort to acquire the knowledge, or the denial that there is an actual lack of knowledge.

Contents

Contents

Sex Education

You can buy books on sex and things
to teach you how to do it
there's pictures and some handy hints
designed to talk you through it
they give you all the proper names
for all your naughty bits
and if your girlfriends big enough
you can prop it on her tits.

The problem with the sex education taught at schools, is that to the average person, it always appears as though he or she is in fact attending the second year of the course, having missed the crucial first year which deals with the more basic but very important points such as: How do you get a date? How do you chat her up? How far do you go on your first date? What if she turns you down? How do you lie to your friends if she turns you down? How do you get another date? Etc...etc...etc...

The questions which girls want asked is not "How many orgasms do you have a week, and are they multiple orgasms?" But rather, "What is an orgasm, and how do you get one?"

Keeping Your Cool

There are guys who are so cool, it's unbelievable. They lose their job....they are cool, they lose their money....they are cool, they smash the car....they are cool. Then comes the ultimate test, and a beautiful girl walks past, and they are as cool as a volcano. They try not to look, but the head stays put. They try to stand straight, but the body has other ideas. They try to keep their tonge and eyes in place, but the wretched things pop out.

Women of course thrive on these reactions, and go to great lengths to get these reactions. They walk around with beautifully shaped bodies, with very little hint of clothing, and when the guy loses his cool and looks at her with his tongue hanging out, she pretends she doesn't know what all the fuss is about, and is amazed that the guy should be looking at her.

So if you want to get your back on such girls, and call their bluff, then all you have to do is to avoid looking at them when they walk past, and pretend you didn't even notice they were there because you were looking at something more interesting like air wizzing past.

This is of course easier said than done, and is to be tried by the very strong willed amongst you.

Keeping Your Cool

Body Language Signals Explained

Men have a habit of either completely misunderstanding a girl's body language signals, or just missing them altogether. It is for this reason that a lot of men are turned down more often than they need to be, and that they always manage to miss those once in a life time opportunities, of a girl actually sending out the 'come on' signal.

So here is a checklist of the signals women use, and their meanings.

She wants you if....

1. she talks to you, touches you or pinches your bottom, etc...

2. she keeps feeling her own body, stroking her legs and waist gently while looking at you.

3. she makes a habit of showing you her tongue gently wetting her lips.

4. she begins to show more of her body, legs etc. than she needs to.

5. Or if you miss the above, she may carry a banner as illustrated.

She Doesn't Want you if....

1. she keeps frowning at you, whilst showing you the nails on her first two fingers.

2. if she tries to avoid you, by hiding in the loo, or just leaving quietly.

3. if she calls her boyfriend, and asks him to beat the hell out of you for harassing her.

Is the girls' Body Language too subtle for men?

The Seduction Techniques

The seduction techniques of men and women, whilst very similar in principle, are usually worlds apart in subtlety.

Women are usually so subtle when it comes to trying to seduce a man that the signal normally flies straight over his head without a glimmer of acknowledgement. Men on the other hand are as subtle as a bull in a china shop.

WOMEN'S METHODS OF SEDUCTION:

1. Just being in the same place at the same time, waiting for a miracle.

2. Casually walking past the man.

3. Concentrating hard, hoping for telepathy to transmit the message.

4. Body language: showing off her assets touching her body, going pink etc.

MEN'S SEDUCTION TECHNIQUES:

1. Approaching her and asking questions like; 'Are you on the pill?'

2. Complimenting her on her figure, then touching it for examination.

3. Missing the formalities, and going straight for the full blow kiss.

4. Practically raping her to show he is interested.

The Seduction

Chatting Up

That is what happens when you forget the most important rule of chatting up. The chat up lines you use are of course very important, but the first rule before the actual chat up line is the observation period. You must observe your victim and her reaction before and more importantly during the time you are trying your chat up line.

Before the chat up.

Watch her carefully for a little while, having decided that she is the one you want to go for, observe her little habits and ways and likes and dislikes etc. then approach, trying to immitate some of those little habits so that she feels comfortable in your company. Some habits must not of course be immitated. These would include; fixing the bra or stroking the leg etc.

During chatting up

Observe her reaction to every word you say, and repeat or omit from your next line, depending on whether the expression on her face resembles that of being delighted or disgusted.

It is worth remembering that some women do play hard to get. When a lady says 'NO', she means maybe. When a lady says 'MAYBE' she means yes. When a lady says 'YES' she is no lady, but rather a person some guys would label as 'A sure thing'.

Chatting Up

I chatted up this girl last night
but she never said a word.
I repeated all my questions,
in case she hadn't heard
I thought she might be foreign
or deaf or drunk or loaded
Until I lit a match a bit too close
and the silly bitch exploded.

The Chat Up Lines

The following chat up lines are for those of you who would prefer not to bore your victim into submission by long winded stories, but rather go for the quick snappy lines which leave her wanting more.

1. How would you like your eggs?......Fertilised?

2. I am very sexy, rich and extremely handsome......and what's your excuse for being so irrestable?

3. *I really like you in that dress with all the sparkly bits, I like your hair, I like your eyes. Now can I touch your tits?*

4. *I've been watching you for ages and I think you are really sweet. As long as I have got a face, you'll always have a seat.*

5. How about coming up to my place for a spot of heavy breathing?

The Chat Up Lines

6. Boy: Is it true that women say no when they mean yes, and say yes when they mean no?
Girl: Yes/No
Boy: I thought so, now can I buy you a drink?
Girl: Yes/No
Boy: Good, What would you like?

7. If you take my heart by surprise, don't you think the rest of my body has a right to follow?

8. Boy: Only fools, absolute morons and idiots would respond by saying no to this question: "Can I buy you a drink?"
Girl: No
Boy: Only fools, absolute morons and idiots would say no to the following question: "Will you go out with me?"
Girl: No
Boy: I gave you two chances, and you still gave yourself away!!!!

Then walk away and watch her follow you.

Blind Dates

Whoever discovered the idea of Blind Dates must have been a genious. For some men it means halving the formalities of getting your leg over. Doing away with approaching a girl at the risk of being turned down, trying to find an appropriate chat up line, buying drinks, and asking her on a date. For women however, it is a more traumatic experience. They very often hope for long term relationships with marriage very much in mind.

My blind date was gorgeous
the best that I've seen yet
until he tried to take my knickers home
to prove he'd won the bet

Blind Dates do work, but it is important to find out a litle more about your partner than those arranging the blind date are willing to expose.

When my friend described you
it was as handsome and quite big
she didn't say you picked your nose
had a lisp and wore a wig.

First Date

The first date is usually a very special occasion. It is the time that you feel you know everything, through the television, films, books and magazines, not to mention the valuable sex education taught you by your know it all friend. You will however be in for a shock as a real girl is nothing like what you are used to.

Darling you are blonde
and are as buxom as they come
I'd like to take you home with me
to meet my dear old mum.
All the other girls I've known
just seem so understated
And I find it quite unusual that
you don't have to be inflated.

The most important thing to remember is to act cool at all times, and not to panic through the excitement, thinking that you best try it on incase she is expecting it. However painful...let her wait.

It's your first date she's really tasty
play it cook, don't be too hasty,
take things slowly, sex can wait
at least until the second date.

The Slow Dance

Scientists in America are working on theories which imply that perhaps the reason why most men react in such impulsive way to slow music at discos, and parties, could be connected to a minute case of hypnotic trans initiated at the time of their conception. Thus the sound of slow music becoming like a signal for them to go 'hunting' for sex.

Men at discos, could be sitting down quite happily having a drink and a chat with friends, they could be drunk, they could even have passed out. But the slightest hint of the slow dance starting, and hundreds of them appear out of nowhere, desperately looking for their prey, someone they could hold touch and feel for a few moments without the risk of being arrested for it.

The most astonishing change that occurs to men during the slow dance, however, is their ability to grow extra arms at moments notice. This enables them to play their favourite disco game called "Touch her up, before she catches up".

The Slow Dance: The Disco Game

The Kiss

A good kiss is the most enjoyable activity two people can indulge in without have to undress. Whilst there have been many books written on the art of kissing, some men still believe that all they need for a good kiss is an open mouth and a tongue.

Kissing can be difficult
but you don't have time to quibble
just open wide, stick your tongue inside
and do try not to dribble.

Kissing is a very important way of showing affection. It is not how you kiss, but rather why you kiss. Every kiss should be slightly different according to the mood of the moment. The most important kiss, however is that first kiss; which tells more about you than a whole evening of conversation. It can reveal whether you are passionate, ambitious, a bore, and most important of all, how regularly you visit your dentist.

The first kiss can mean a lot
do you use your tongue or not
If you don't she may not notice
Cause she's passed out from your halitosis.

The Enthusiastic Kiss

Falling In Love

The act of falling in love is marked by certain very obvious transformations in the appearance and actions of those actually experiencing this phenomina.

SIGNS OF FALLING IN LOVE:

1. Life continues, but in slow motion, the lovers flowing in the air and seeing everything from a completely different and wierd angle.

2. The brain leaves on an extended holiday.

3. The mouth adopts a constant smile.

4. The legs become wobbly due to lack of blood circulation, being needed else where.

5. The blank glare of the eyes show that though the lights are on, no one is at home.

6. Finally the shape of the body changes. Fats round the waist disappear inside, allowing other parts to project out further.

WHAT MAKES MEN & WOMEN FALL IN LOVE.

WOMEN: A man's potential, intelligence, sense of humour, strength, sensitivity, and personality.

MEN: A woman's looks, hair, legs, breasts, lips, waiste, eyes and sex appeal.

Falling in Love

Is Sex out of the Question?

That is probably the most important question lingering in the mind, from the moment a man sees a girl, during the chat up and conversations and right through the first date, to the time she finally gives in.

> *It's your first date she's really tasty*
> *play it cool, don't be too hasty*
> *take things slowly, sex can wait*
> *at least until the second date*

Most men however can not wait till the second date. They need to know the answer to that important question.

So if you really want to know, but are too afraid to ask; here are a few hints you should look out for, in search of the answer:

She will if...
1. she mentions money

2. she mentions your small bottom, and how it turns her on

3. she invites you back to her place for a coffee, whilst touching your legs

4. she mentions she doesn't wear underwear

She won't if she...
1. talks about marriage

2. honeymoons

3. wedding dresses

4. love

Will she or Won't She?

Romance – A beginners checklist

The word 'ROMANCE' has originated from the fifteenth century by a philosopher who observed a certain species of ants found in the outskirts of Rome. These ants would always travel in pairs, eat in pairs, sleep in pairs and die in pairs. They were very emotionally and sexually attached to each other.

In today's language, romance means being throughful in a special way towards your loved one. Whilst it is something an individual is born with, it is nevertheless easily acquired if needs be.

Don't start getting frantic
about being romantic
It's a skill and it has to be learned
if you nakedly tangle
by the light of a candle
your balls could get seriously burned

Romantic Gestures:

1. Wake her up before making love.

2. Get her name right specially during sex.

3. Surprise her by occasionally being a little more considerate.

Romance

The First Time

Women think you know it all
but that's not true I swear
I knew I had to stick it in
What I didn't know was where

The first time you make love will mark a very special occasion in your life, leaving memories which linger on for the rest of your life. Now, there are two ways one can go through this experience; there is the proper way, and then there is the silly way.

The Proper Way:

1. The person sharing this important experience has to be a very special person in your life.

2. The mood has to be right. The atmosphere filled with love and passion.

3. The venue has to be carefully planned, and very romantic, or at least comfortable.

The Silly Way

1. Sharing the experience with anyone who is willing, drunk and available.

2. Pubs are closed, Football is not on TV, and she is awake...So the mood is right. The latter to some people is not necessarily that important.

3. Where you do it is irrelevant, as long as she has no time to change her mind, before you actually get there. The safest bet therefore always turns out to be the back of the car, where you haven't even got room to swing a condom in.

The First Time

Only foods, complete idiots and absolute morans would look at page..4......12.4

Love Bites

Love bite is a technique adopted by man through his observation of the mating habits of animals in the wild.

The male lion, during sex, bites hold of his female companion, preventing her from slipping away. Man has perfected the technique by replacing the use of teeth with a subtle sucking action.

The question why people give love bites, is not as interesting as the following two questions which need to be asked;

1. why do people show their love bites?

2. why do people pretend they are hiding their love bites.

People who show their love bites, are taking advantage of the free advertising space on their necks to tell the world what great lovers they are, to be able to give such enjoyment to their partners to make them lose control, and leave such unsightly marks.

"IAM A GREAT LOVER AND I DON'T MIND TELLING YOU".

Those who try to pretend they are doing their best to hide their love bites, are giving out the same message, but with a little more modesty.

I AM A GREAT LOVER, THOUGH I DON'T LIKE TO BRAG ABOUT IT".

Love Bites : The DIY Technique

LOVE is alive and kicking when...

LOVE is alive and kicking when...

1. You have an affair with someone else, and actually feel guilty about it.

2. The mention of the word "Marriage", does not bring out the cold sweat, but is considered as a possibility for the future.

3. You get her name right everytime, and notice any changes in her appearance since the last time you saw her. Subtle changes like having her head shaved.

4. You stop drinking beer, move on to spirits, and even pretend you don't like Football.

5. You notice when you start to smell, and try to cover it up.

6. You only eat onions if it is included in the price, and she is eating it with you.

7. When in conversation with her, you hear her voice, and remember what she has said for at least ten minutes.

8. You start to look at other women only when you are on your own.

Do Men have any control over their eyes or their actions when confronted by a beautiful woman?

....................NO....................

How often have you found yourself in front of the television, watching a foreign film with subtitles; when all of a sudden the woman in the film begins to undress. How many of you can honestly say that you carried on reading the subtitles, so as not to miss the plot. if you really have, then you are either a lier or just a fool.

This is a weakness that men are born with, and many have been made to look like fools trying to conceal it. Particularly when accompanied by their loved ones, to places where the problem is at its highest intensity, such as the beach etc.

Men go to great lengths to con their way into looking in the direction of the cause of the problem. They may, all of a sudden feel the urge to start exercising that painful stiff neck, thus turning their head back and forth towards the desired direction. They may even send their dog or child in the direction of the girl, to fetch something, and look on pretending to be just a caring responsible adult.

Whatever trick men play, they play because their brain is no longer in control, and the eyes are on auto pilot.

I Wasn't Looking at her...

Can I Come In For A 'Coffee'?

The word 'Coffee' has in the past decade or two taken on a completely new meaning. It is no longer a word used to describe a hot drink consumed for relaxation, but rather a word used to suggest rampant sex in the privacy of ones home.

As sad as it may sound, going back to her place for a coffee, is for most guys the raison de'tare of taking the girl out. But it's crucial to leave the idea for her to suggest, so as not to appear pushy, which is a complete turn off for most women.

If you feel she is too slow, and may not even suggest the idea, then how about dropping the odd hint, like breaking into nursery rhymes:

> *Jack and Jill went down the diary*
> *Jack got out his big fat hairy*
> *Jill said 'Blimey what a whopper'*
> *Lets go home and do it propper.*

Finally it is important to note that being asked in for a coffee, does not necessarily mean that all is well.

> *She asked if I'd come back for coffee*
> *I thought we might end up in bed*
> *But I got stuck on the sofa with granny*
> *I'm not fussy, I shagged her instead.*

Foreplay

Foreplay as is believed by some guys, is not another name for an orgy. It is in fact the preparation for the special act of making love. It is like the starter before the main course. If you are one of those unlucky ones who gets full up with the starter and can't handle the main course, see the section on Premature Ejaculation.

For the rest of you here are some helpful pointers:

Caressing breasts can be quite dicey
make sure you hands aren't icy
Please don't twiddle – That's no no
You're not tuning a radio

If you fancy sex one night
please do try to be polite
It's only fair for goodness sake
to check the girl is still awake

Oral sex if you should doubt it,
Doesn't mean talking about it
and the other thing that you should know
is one's supposed to suck not blow

Foreplay

The Most sought after Parts of the body

The Parts of the Body Sensitive to the touch

Where is the 'G' Spot?

If you are one of those very considerate men who wish to make your woman feel extatic and uncontrollable in the bedroom; we have some good news and some bad news for you.

The Good News: Women have been created with some very special points on their body, where they are ultra sensitive, and should anyone find, touch or caress these spots, they may experience seeing a woman's extacy.

The Bad News: You will never find them. Apart from a few accidental tries, no one has yet been able to find these spots, or at least relocate them a second time.

The 'G' Spot: is the most searched for treasure. The G stands for George who discovered this spot for the first time, in the 15th century. It was at that moment that also the phrase "BY GEORGE' was first uttered.

We suggest that when practising to locate this spot, one should begin with the basic exercise illustrated on the opposite page.

The Clitoris:

> *If you can find the clitoris*
> *this turns girls on a treat*
> *But it's not on the upper arms*
> *and thights or the feet.*
> *I've searched about for hours*
> *but I've never found a thing*
> *It is somewhere between the naval*
> *and that funny piece of string?*

Size Isn't Everything

Size isn't everything,
that simply isn't true.
Can you ever recall the time
when a woman said to you,
"You are really great between the sheets
delivered with a snigger,
"You are really great I promise you,
but I wish your dick was bigger"
They are never satisfied
with the dimensions of your member,
they always wish it extra large
you know, just to remember.
But has the thought occurred to them,
a though not too uncanny,
that the fault may actually lie with them,
and that they need a tighter fanny!!!

Size Isn't Everything

Sex Positions

We were lying face to face
when he got bored and moved
I don't mean to whine, I quite like 69
but the scenery could be improved.

This has never happened to me before

This is without question, everyman's nightmare. It is like going to war, and trying to kill tne enemy with a sword made out of sponge.

But then, you knew that, because it is something which happens to the best of men, at some point in their lives. This together with disputes about the size of a man's genitals, are probably the two most effective ego shatterers. That is why, no matter how many times a man finds himself with a sponge sword, he always insists, that its the first time.

The cause can be anything one wishes to use as an excuse; too much drink, stress, or even 'I must still be in love with Jenny'

The cure is simple..........continence!!!

For those men who wish to keep their ego in tact during such embarrassing time, you could try the following line.

"As much as I want you right now, you mean more to me than just a one night stand. I want it to be very special, that's why I am willing to wait."

"Anyway...Do you think the shop will exchange these condoms with some starch?"

This has never happened to me before

Premature Ejaculation

Premature Ejaculation is without doubt one of the most serious sexual problems men could suffer from, without even realising anything was wrong. The intensity of the problem for some is measured in seconds, and for those very unlucky ones even in fractions of a second. If you suffer from it, don't worry because there is a cure......just give up sex.

For those women who have planned and waited for that special someone to make love to, discover to their horor that it was hardly worth waiting for, cause he suffers from PME, here is a little suggestion which might help.

> *When you get to bed at last*
> *if he's getting there too fast*
> *stop mid stroke, and loudly shriek*
> *I need to buy pile cream this week*
> *then scratch a bit, it never fails*
> *takes the wind out of his sails.*

Premature Ejaculation

Premature Ejaculation

Premature Ejaculation,
not a thing to happen,
like boarding on a train to Wales,
but getting off at Clapham.
The more you try to preserve
and reach your destination
you'll create more hold ups on the way
that'll stunt your situation.
So take a breath and just relax,
don't dwell on past performance,
'cause if she truly loves you
it won't be of great importance
be confident around her
to alleviate your fear
then try to do it all again,
and watch your problem disappear!!

Premature Ejaculation: Passing the buck

Premature Ejaculation...The Cure

Premature Ejaculation is a very serious problem, but not one which science has left unresolved.

The following solutions to the problem have been collated from the laboratories of some of the leading scientists who are currently researching on the problem at hand.

1. The Rope Remedy:
As illustrated on opposite page, it is a very simple set up. It involves a rope tied at one end to the testicles, and at the other end to the neck. During moments when a premature ejaculation is about to happen, the guy raises his head, thus causing a slight burning pain, accompanied by a quiet scream, this is usually enough to take the mind off its tracks, giving a well needed recovery period, therefore lengthening

the duration of sex.

2. The Mirror method
In this method, a mirror is kept handy during sex, and occasionally propped up against the girl's face. The thought of one making love to ones self does disengage the brain and reduce one's excitement at that point.

We must stress however that this method for some guys can have the opposite effect, thus encouraging premature ejaculation.

Premature Ejaculation...The Cure

You Know she is faking her orgasm when........

Whether a woman fakes her orgasms or not, is something majority of men would rather not question in case they discovered that she has been all along, and that they are not in fact the stud they thought, women go wild for, but rather a pathetic creature with a problem who needs to be patronised.

So for those of you who would prefer not to ask her, but still like to know, there is a simple checklist to help you.

1. In the middle of lovemaking, and just before the moment it sound as though she is about to have an orgasm, stop and take away the magazine she has been reading. If she says "Oi I was reading that", then she was faking it.

2. If her panting, groaning and screaming are in tune, or sound like a familiar song, then she can't be concentrating enough on the job at hand, and must therefore be faking it. Or else she really likes the song playing on her personal stereo.

3. A rule of thum, which is usually very accurate is: Stop at randam, and record her response, if everytime you stop she says "Mmmmm You were wonderful", then she is faking it. If she says "Don't stop", then she isn't. However, if she says "Don't stop", hours after lovemaking has finished, it is possible that she may have fallen asleep, and missed most of the excitement.

She must be faking her orgasm if...

Before Sex

This is the time designated to women. It is a time when men are like putty in a woman's hand. They will beg, shout scream and agree to almost anything a woman asks of them.

It is a time when women realise that they pull the strings, and can have fun just humiliating men.

Then finally after many hours of begging, he succeeds, they go to bed, they have sex, he finishes, and then begins his designated time, when he's satisfied, but she wants more. Not that much more, but just enought to write home about.

Our sex life isn't boring
He won't leave me alone
he's at it while I'm cooking
or while I'm on the phone .
he likes it every hour
he doesn't like to miss
So I apologise mum, in advance
if you can't read this.

After Sex

After sex the relationship takes on a new phase. Now the guy begins to act cool, his objective has been fulfilled. The woman on the other hand becomes very emotional and attached, wanting to find out more about each other on route to a long and happy relationship.

When you've finished having sex
and you're feeling quite relaxed
don't go dropping off to sleep
though you're tired and overtaxed
keep the conversation light
play a little game
ask some simple questions
or at least find out her name.

The guy at this point usually loses interest for a while, and forgets all his manners he had before he got his way.

The perfect lover after sex
will first turn out the lamp
then allow her to kiss you
hand her some tissue
and sleep in the bit that got damp.

How was it for you?

Why is this the most popular question asked by men after sex?
Why do they need to ask? What the hell do they care anyway?

The answer is very simple, men after sex feel drained and
need to boost their ego. They ask the question, but know the
answer already. If one day a woman decides to tell the truth,
it would certainly shatter the man, but he will recover soon
enough to act the little schoolboy that he is at heart, and say
"Well you weren't that great either..Na Na Na Na."

When you've finished making love
and he lies back and scratches
and asks you if he lit your fire
just lean over and hand him the matches

How was it for you?

Women's Sexual desires/Needs

As unlikely as it may sound, women too have their sexual desires which need to be fulfilled. Women don't however make a lot of fuss about this. They are either content with what they get, however unsatisfactory, or they just lie through their teeth for the sake of the man's fragile ego. It is because of this that men quite understandably let it slip from their minds, that women matter too.

Women then either go through many years of frustration, or they resort to other means.

> *He never has a headache*
> *He's responsive to my touch*
> *when I buy an outfit,*
> *He doesn't enquire, how much?*
> *His stamina is incredible,*
> *He'll stay with me to the end*
> *A reliable vibrator is*
> *a single girls best friend*

So if you are concerned about your partners sexual needs, let her talk about them, let her explain, but tell her to hurry, cause you want to make love, and haven't got time for all this nonsense.

What Is an Orgasm?

The word orgasm originates from the word organ. Orgasm being the purpose of the male's organ. Unfortunately however, somewhere along the line, the male organ stopped being used for the purpose it was intended, and took on a whole new purpose for life, adopting a mind of his own.

It is because of this that a number of men have still not witnessed an orgasm. They are very kindly reassured by their considerate women who say, "It's not you, I never have an orgasm, I still enjoyed it though." What women do for the sake of a man's ego is beyond me.

Anyhow, for those of you who have never witnessed an orgasm, here is what happens, so don't panic and dial 999.

Her muscles contract making her bite, scratch, stick her nails in your skin, squash them between her legs, scream, pant, laugh, cry, shout, sing and then she starts havig an orgasm.

Meanwhile for you, if you have ever needed a favour, this is the time to ask her.

Witnessing an Orgasm for the First Time.

My period is late....................

The dreaded words that every man is subjected to at some point in his life. It's like having a bucket of burning coal poured over your head, but not feeling a thing. Just the thought of it was enough to make you num.

It is amazing how a man changes when subjected to these words. Panic can wait, the first job at hand for most men is figuring out how to kill that baby.

> *When I told you I was pregnant*
> *all you did was grin*
> *then you send me off to run a bath*
> *and handed me the gin!!*

The insensitivity of a man really shows through when in this position. They say things like:

• Well do you know who the father is?

• How can you be so stupid?

• OK you've got me...I'll pay half the abortion fees.

• Stop crying, of course I'll marry you, but lets just get rid of the kid first.

• If this is a trap, I am not falling for it. So you are on your own.

Then after all that the period finally arrives, and the false alarm is set to rest by his final words:

"Darling... You know I would have married you. I just wanted it to be special."

What if I was Pregnant?

Getting Pregnant

They were jostling at the starting line,
preparing for the chase,
Waiting for his climax,
to initiate the race.
The urgency unbearable,
his dick was having fun.
then all at once they all shot forth
as if shot from a gun.
Swimming with Olympic skills,
they swam the dark red tunnel,
through a hole far up ahead,
shaped like a vast red funnel.
Sammy sperm was winning,
he was heading up the pack,
his little tail wiggling
he sped past Liz and Jack.

Getting Pregnant

Then dimly further up ahead,
and much to his surprise,
he spied a little tiny egg,
and scarce believed his eyes.
His speed increased, he bobbed and weaved
and continued very fast,
his objective laying just in front,
he arrived there at long last.
Peeping in then creeping in,
they joined as if were guided,
then swelled and heaved
then once again,
and instantly divided.
This process then continued,
for roughly nine months maybe,
and then the egg and Sammy sperm
became a healthy baby.

Contraceptions For The Man

Science with all its glory is proud to announce the arrival of yet another variation to their original Contraception for men:

The Condom

To take stock of what we now have on the market at our disposal in the way of contraceptives for men, here is a list:

1. Standard condoms

2. Coloured condoms

3. Flavoured condoms

4. Illuminous condoms

5. Musical condoms

6. Ribbed condoms

7. Multi fingured condoms

8. Edible condoms

9. Reusable condoms

10. Vasectomy. This being a very unpopular choice due to the childish jokes anyone who has had a vasectomy is subjected to. Jokes like: Why are men who have had vasectomies like Christmas Trees. Because the balls hanging from them are for decoration only.

Contraceptions For the Man

Contraceptions For the Woman

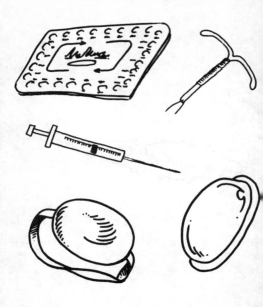

An Idiots guide to The correct use of Contraceptions For Women

The Cap: is not intended to go on the end of your willy, as those of you have discovered to your relief, after many hours of worry about why your willy is so small for a tight grip. It is in fact intended to fit inside the vagina, rather like a condom for women.

The Diaphram is widely used
the 'cap' as it is called
if you're wise, you'll check the size
too small, and you'll go bald.

The Sponge: No wrong again. The sponge is not intended to be used to wipe around the girl's genitals and legs after sexual intercourse. It fits in the girl's vagina to stop your wicked sperms getting any further.

The Coil: As seen in the illustration opposite, it looks like a fishing tackle, but is not intended to be used as one to catch the naughty little sperms that have got away. It acts more like a fishing net used to catch sperms going into dangerous waters.

The Pill: Men's favourite. Taken once a day. Day after day after day, just for a few seconds of sex now and then.

The Injection: This really is the last straw, and raises the question, "Would men still crave sex if they had to have an injection beforehand?"

Contraceptions

Contraceptions

Contraception: the Choice

She sat depressed and half undressed
trying to understand
why of every form of birth control
only one was for the man
all they every need is a condom and cream
the simplicity of which
must be every womans dream.
Yet do they every use it?
they hardly ever will
after every fumble in the dark
they say 'you on the pill?'
they just go ahead
puffing and red,
and accept no responsibility
they wriggle and writhe
and expect a few sighs
to maintain their macho virtility.
She imagines a chap
inserting a cap
through the hole in the end of his willy
then imagines his toil
and his pain from a coil
the emergency result looking silly.
A smile starts to race
the whole width of her face
but she still sits and ponders why
out of all contraceptory birth control means
only one can be used by a guy.

Contraception: The choice

Can I have a pack of large Condoms

Instructions On a Condom

Instructions on a condom
may be bard to understand
but 'organ' means your willy
and not your girlfriends baby grand

The complexity of the use of the condom is only the second most popular reason why some guys are still reluctant to use one. The most popular reason is that it costs too much. It is likely that those guys are perhaps judging the cost with the few seconds they actually use it for. Then granted it does become as costly as £248 per minute.

If you can't afford lots of condoms
but you don't want to worry and doubt
with not to much trouble the usage you'll double
if you turn the whole thing inside out.

An Englishman goes to the chemist and asks for a pack of three condoms, and explains its for Monday, Wednesday and Friday.

An Italian comes along and asks for a pack of seven condoms; Monday, Tuesday, Wednesday, Thursday etc.

An Irishman comes along and to the amazement of the shop assistant asks for a pack of twelve condoms. When asked he explains that they are for; January, February, March etc.

Use a condom before its too late.

A.I.D.S....It will never happen to me

There was a time when Syphilis and Gonorrhoea were the sexually transmitted diseases people felt guilty about when they practised unsafe sex. Nowdays, with AIDS very much in the forefront, Syphilis and Gonorrhoea seem like a breath of fresh air, a mild cold or even a little pimple on the face.

AIDS is the real McCoy...It does not joke, it does not show his face, an it does not hurt.....IT KILLS.

THOSE WHO NEED NOT WORRY ABOUT AIDS:

1. Those who enjoy playing Russian Roulett, and are prepared for death.

2. Those who are so desperate for one sexual experience (without protection) that they would gladly give their life for.

If however you do not fall in any of the above two categories, you should take the following precautions to avoid catching AIDS.

1. No sex without a Condom. However inconvenient, remember its nothing compared to trying to have sex after death.

2. No oral sex.

3. No deep french kissing.

If in doubt always remember the sentence which has become the epitaph for many like you:

"...And I thought it would never happen to ME."

Pre-Menstrual Tension PMT

A girl who is Pre-Menstrual
will argue, snap and sob
If you are wise, you'll sympathise
or you might get a smack in the gob.

Men bless them, are so thick when it comes to understanding women. PMT comes round every month, and yet everytime it comes round, they need to ask: "What's the matter with you?" Some men simply forget about the woman's monthly condition, whilst others are just thick.

I fancied this young guy called Michael he said "come
round to have sex if you like"
I said "I can't, I've got my Menstrual Cycle"
he said, "What's sex got to do with your bike"

Men are kids at heart, and always want what they can't have. Sex during the woman's menstrual cycle is no exception. So here is a suggestion for the woman with this problem.

The time of month come round again,
when you are feeling mean and cruel
He wants sex, you don't,
but you must humour the old fool.
May I suggest a perfect way to win this little fight
suggest a little soixante-neuf
then take hold of it and BITE.

Pre-Menstrual Tension PMT

Pre-Menstrual Depression

Pre-Menstrual Depression is the anxiety and depression experienced by the man during the woman's monthly cycle, at which time she is unable to make love, and he for some unknown reason feels horniest. Thus creating a situation where the man attempts every means available to him, just for a bit of what he preceives as his reason for living. The most obvious symptoms during this period are:

1. Constant begging.

2. Uncontrollable crying sessions accompanied by talk of suicide.

3. The unmistakeable SULK.

> *If you are craving chocolate*
> *and alcohol as well*
> *If you're feeling bloated*
> *and your poor old ankles swell*
> *If you're shouting at the kids*
> *just cope the best you can*
> *we could put it down to PMT*
> *but darling, you're a man.*

For those women who find the symptoms too unbareable, try the following:

> *That time of months come round again*
> *when you are feeling mean and cruel*
> *he wants sex, you don't,*
> *but you must humour the old fool..*
> *May I suggest a perfect way*
> *to win this little fight;*
> *suggest a little soixante-neuf,*
> *then take hold of it and BITE!!!*

Pre-Menstrual Depression

Pre-Menstrual Tension PMT

PMT is the nature's way of helping the woman get even with the man for the inconsiderate, selfish little creature that he normally is.

It is a slight transformation of character the woman goes through to help her put the man in his place.

A wise man plans ahead of time; having carefully marked his diary with the possible start and finish days, he should then find a reason to be suddenly called away for that period. A business trip or Grandmother dying are two possible excuses worth trying if you have not already run out of grandmothers.

Otherwise you should sit down, shut up and do as you are told.

Question: Why does it take five women with PMT to change a light bulb?

Answer: It just does....O.K.?

Pre-Menstrual Tension PMT

How Do you tell if she is still a virgin?

You ask her....

If she says 'yes', then she isn't a virgin.

If she says 'no' then she must be.

This is why you were unable to spot the virgin out of the two girls on the opposite page.

The reason for this is very simple. A virgin would be reluctant to allow anyone to jump to conclusions, that the reason for her virginity is that there is something wrong with her, or that she is undesirable. She therefore brags about situations and experiences she has never had. If she isn't a virgin, then she would like to pretend that she is still pure and untouched, incase she is confronted by one of the many men who prefer virgins. With the knowledge of the experience to fall back on if needs be.

Virginity is like a bubble...One prick and its gone.

A virgin is a lovely thing
she's pure and she's rare and she's sweet
She'll be filled full of fright
she will probably wear white
and undoubtedly bleed on the sheet.

Spot the Virgin

Women and Marriage

Marriage has always been a subject raised in conversations, hinted at, and discussed more often by women than by men. Perhaps the reason for this is the fact that men are cowards when it comes to commitments and long term plans. This coupled with the allergy which most men suffer from; bringing them out in cold sweat by just the mention of the word 'marriage', has made it very difficult for women to raise the subject. They have therefore perfected a language of their own just for this.

Women are suggesting marriage when they talk about the following....

1. Their monthly cycle being late.

2. Honeymoons & Wedding dresses.

3. Kids & the recent increase in child benefit.

4. Friends' weddings.

5. I bet you look nice in a Tuxedo.

6. My parents want to see me married before they die.

7. So and so said we make a lovely couple.

8. I love wearing jewelery on my fingures.

9. I don't believe in sex before marriage.

Painful Sexual Fantacies

Men's Sexual Fantacies

Men as already suggested are by nature a very randy bunch, and it doesn't take much to get them started.

Most men fall into four categories, according to the effort needed to get them turned on.

1. The first category which counts for 75% of men need only the mention of the word 'women', which is normally enough to push them close to their climax.

2. The second category, 10% of men, need a little more convincing. Here, adding another word to the original, so that it becomes 'Naked woman', normally does the trick.

3. The third category, which count for a staggering 12% of men actually need a jump start in the form of fantacies. These fantacies may include:

   a) Friendly nurses.

   b) Friendly women in authority.

   c) More than one woman at the same time.

   d). Dressing up in wierd clothes.

(We strongly recommend that those who are turned on by the latter seek help).

4. Then we have the fourth category, the final 2% of men, whose batteries don't need jump leads, they need replacing. The components of the battery having stood idol for a while have ceased up.

Women's Sexual Fantacies

Women too, have sexual fantacies. But unlike men whose fantacies are sex only related, womens' also take on board all the other emotional qualities they wish in their men. These qualities which women fantasise about are:

1. Being stranded on a desert island with a strong romantic hunk, who has no hope of leaving.

2. Men in uniforms. Here we have to point out that there is a line to be drawn, where pilot's uniform is in, and a dustman's uniform is out.

3. Passion and vitality in men.

> *If you're good together*
> *you'll have passion, you'll have heat*
> *you'll have bite marks on your buttocks*
> *and a scorch mark on the sheet.*

4. Making love in the most unusual places, particularly where they might be caught.

> *We had to do it everywhere*
> *passion made us weak*
> *well we've been banned from the stores*
> *'though I think they've got a cheek.*

5. Being watched, stripped with the eyes and lusted over by many men.

Women's Sexual Fantacies

The Characteristics of a creep

MIRROR

Proven turn-offs for Women

Women are a lot more fussy about men, than men are about women. The following proven turn offs, has been extensively researched and well documented. If more than five relate to you, then there is cause for concern, and you need to consider changing you ways if you want to stand any chance of impressing the opposite sex.

Women hate the following:

1. Men who fancy themselves more than their women.

2. Men who appear to have half of their face lifted, thus giving a constant raised eyebrow, and a lopsided smile.

3. Men who show off or appear to show off any part of their body which is actually not as sexy as they think. A hairy chest and a medallion is a good example here.

4. Men who through self indulgence allow their body to take on the shape of a ripe avacado.

5. Men who are very attached to their socks, and tend not to take them off just for anyone.

6. Men who are loud, pretencious, and ignorant of others perceptions of them.

Two-Timing

Twotiming With Indiscrete Tactics

T W I T

Those guys who indulge in a little bit of indiscrete two-timing, are usually in desperate need of an ego boost, with the aim of being branded Casanova very much in mind.

Others who are subtle and discrete about it, are two-timing for genuine reasons, and are discrete because of the fear of being found out and thus losing their loved one.

It is this fear that causes the two-timer to act in the most peculiar way, thus providing hints, which anyone suspecting their loved one should look out for.

> *Buying coal can be sign*
> *that your wife has started cheating*
> *especially if you get your warmth*
> *from gas fired central heating.*

Other actions which give a two timer away are:

• A sudden desire to make love more often than normal.

• A sudden transformation into the most considerate, loving partner ever lived.

• A desire to have baths straight after coming home, also washing every bit of clothing.

• Buying presents, flowers, etc.

• Working at odd times, without leaving a contact number.

• Staying with friends more often than normal.

Having An Affair

The Problem with Toy Boys

To make love to a younger man
is really quite the fashion
they've usually got hair and teeth
and lots of youthful passion
They'll smother you with kisses
you don't have to play it cool
you just have to write Excuse me notes
to get them out of school.

Some women prefer the mature experienced men who
dominate and control the sexual experience, others don't.
They prefer playing games with little boys, however frustrating
it may turn out to be.

Stood behind the bike sheds
we were doing fine
he told me that he'd show me his
if I would show him mine
I whipped up my pinafore
and dropped my knickers quick
he whipped out his latin prep
I WAS hoping for his dick

Burying the LOVE gracefully

Don't You Love me anymore?

When one of the two partners falls out of love, it is the beginning of a war, with the other persons pride and ego very much at stake. No one wants to be known by others to have been dumped. They therefore go through a phase of fighting and insulting each other, just to be able to say that they had the last word.

> *If your girlfriend dumps you*
> *revenge can be divine*
> *say that she's one of three*
> *You gave her V.D.*
> *and your AIDS test came back borderline*

Insulting and hurting a man is of course a lot easier because of their more fragile ego.

> *If you are feeling mean and cruel*
> *tell him you don't like his tool*
> *it's amazing how he flinches*
> *when you point out that he lacks 3 inches.*

Breaking Up/Making Up

The actual breaking up and making up of a relationship for some couples is what keeps the love alive. If you are amongst such people, it is worth noting that certain insensitivities can leave scars and thus making the making up that much more difficult.

Being insensitive however is the man's favourite tool for breaking up, in most cases coming very naturally to him, thus hurting with intent to breaking up for a bit on the side with the pretense of not realising the insensitivity.

I know that I'm not perfect
there's very few who are
he much preferred the garden
the football and his car
well now he's gone and left me
and the memories cause me pain
but it was the end
when he directed his friend
back to fulham
on my varicose vein.

The making up is also very exciting because of the anger and hurt still in mind, yet couples desperately trying to go along with tact so as not to jeopardise the fun of making up.

When it comes to making up
you may be feeling miffed
here's what you shouldn't say
if you want to heal the rift
no matter how annoyed you are
don't say what you are feeling
can I read for a bit, are you in, was that it?
are you going to paint the ceiling?

You are becoming a pervert when....

You Know You Are Getting
Desperate When....

Watching the actions of a desperate man suffer from the withdraw symptoms of not having had sex for a while would probably make the saddest wild life programme ever seen.

The SIGNS OF GETTING DESPERATE:

1. You go to great lengths to con women into stretching or bending over, so as to provide a glimps of what certain parts of her body look like.

2. At parties, discos and other public places, you feel this urge to stand at the bottom of the stairs, casually looking up at the steps and things.

3. Window shopping becomes your favourite pass time; particularly those half finished with the old undressed mannequin still waiting to be dressed.

4. Finally everyday objects around the home begin to remind you of women and thus take on a special beauty. These objects, according to the extent of the desperation may include: Saucepan tops, melons, oranges, toilet rolls etc...

<u>You know you are getting desperate when.....</u>

The Battle of the sexes

Why do women put up with Men?

Beats me...What I do know, however, is that I too tend to keep a lot of old junk, incase one day, I may find a good use for them.

Men think they are superior
in the boardroom or the sack
We've sent the buggers to the moon
And don't ask me why – brought them back
We've cooked for them, we've cleaned for them
We've given them our heart
then they take you to bed
they take hold of your head
push it under the duvet and fart.

QUESTION: What do you call that useless piece of skin at the end of a penis?

ANSWER: MAN

To avoid being sexist, we have to include the following entitled "MEN ON WOMEN"

Women are funny old creatures
they all want to be pampered and kissed
they nag and they moan
well I'd rather stay at home
and just settle for one off the wrist.

When He Says....He means....

When he says: "Don't you love me?"
He means: Why the hell won't you have sex with me?

When he says: I hope you don't think I am trying to chat you up"
He means: Please don't run away, let me talk to you for a while.

When he says: "Can I buy you a drink?"
He means: Any chance of having sex with me later?

When he says: "I didn't have an affair..Nothing happened."
He means: She wouldn't let me.

When he says: "To me sex is not that important"
He means: I think of nothing else but sex.

When he says: "She is frigid"
He means: She turned me down.

When he says: "You have got lovely legs"
He means: Boy you are ugly.

When he says: "Of course I'll be careful."
He means: Don't talk to me right now.

When he says: This has never happened to me before"
He means: Oh shit...not again.

When he says: "I want an open relationship."
He means: I want to sleep around, until I find someone I like.

When he says: "What is the point of getting married?"
He means: I don't love you enough to marry you.

When he says....He means....

When he says: "Can I come in for a coffee?"
He means: Go on, let me come in and have sex with you.

When he says: "I like reading adult magazines, they have very interesting articles."
He means: I am a pervert, and I only look at the pictures.

When he says: "Can I have this slow dance?"
He means: I want to touch your body.

When he , he means....

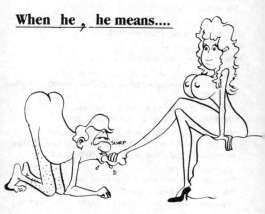

SLURP

When she says....She means....

When she says:
"Not tonight darling, I have a headache
"She means: We either both enjoy making love, or you are not getting it anymore.

When she says:
"Lets go somewhere quiet"
She means: Just because I am desperate, doesn't mean I want anyone else seeing me with you.

When she says: "He is not my type"
She means: I don't think the bastard fancies me.

When she says: "Isn't that a lovely baby?"
She means: I want to have your baby.

When she says: "I trust you"
She means: You fool with me, and I'll kill you.

When she says: "I love you too much as a friend"
She means: Just because I talk to you, doesn't mean, I want to sleep with you.

When she says: "He's got a lovely personality"
She means: He's a nice guy, but boy is he ugly"

When she says: "I wish I could cuddle you all night"
She means" I wish you didn't have such a short fuse, and that lovemaking lasted a little longer than thirty seconds.

When she says: "My period is late"
She means: Let's see what it takes to get you to marry me.
When she says: "I am on a diet"
 She means" Compliment me on my gorgous body, you fool.

The Idiots word Dictionary

I.Q: Just a couple of the letters of the alphabet.

Peacock: An under developed male's sexual organs.

Oral Sex: Talking dirty.

Sophistication: A rare abnormality.

Accessible: Someone who can use a Credit Card.

Adder: A calculator.

Foreplay: An orgy.

Forefathers: Someone whose mum was a bit of a raver.

Etiquette: Before being admitted to certain posh places, it is necessary to get a ticket.

Sexual Etiquette: Paying for sex.

Blockhead: Someone with a solid character.

Ageless: An unborn child.

Offish: The place of work of a person with a lisp.

Preconceive: Foreplay.

Adhere: Bill Boards.

Fettish: Slightly overweight.

Rabbet: A cudly little animal with long ears.

Plato: The word that usually comes before an Italian dish. e.g., A Plato Spaghetti.

Full of Beans: Someone with whom one should not share a lift.

Two chances, and you still gave yourself away.

OTHER TITLES AVAILABLE FROM IDEAS UNLIMITED (PUBLISHING)

Please send me (postage free)

☐ copy/copies of "WELL HUNG" ISBN1–871964–07–5 (96 pages A5) Full Colour @ £2.99

☐ copy/copies of "THE BODY LANGUAGE SEX SIGNALS" ISBN 1–871964–06–7 @ £2.50"

☐ copy/copies of "100 Chat Up Lines" ISBN 1–871964–00–8 (128 pages A7) @ £1.99

☐ copy/copies of "Of course I Love You" ISBN 1–871964–01–6 (96 pages A6) @ £1.99

☐ copy/copies of "The Idiots Handbook of Love & Sex" ISBN 1–871964–08–3 (128 pages A7 size) @ £1.99

☐ copy/copies of "The Beginners Guide to Kissing" ISBN 1–871964–02–4 (64 pages A5) @ £2.50

☐ copy/copies of "Tips for a Successful Marriage" ISBN 1–871964–03–2 (64 pages A5) @ £2.50

☐ copy/copies of "The Joy of Fatherhood" ISBN 1–871964–04–0 (64 pages A5) @ £2.50

☐ copy/copies of "Office Hanky Panky" ISBN 1–871964–05–9 (64 pages A5) @ £2.50

I have enclosed a cheque/postal order for £_____ made payable to Ideas Unlimited (Publishing)

Name: _____

Address: _____

Fill in the coupon and send it with your payment to: Ideas Unlimited (Publishing) PO Box 125, Portsmouth PO1 4PP

AVAILABLE FROM IDEAS UNLIMITED

...e (postage free)

...pies of "WELL HUNG" ISBN1–871964–07–5
...ges A5) Full Colour @ £2.99

...copies of "THE BODY LANGUAGE SEX SIGNALS"
...N 1–871964–06–7 @ £2.50

...copy/copies of "100 Chat Up Lines"
...ISBN 1–871964–00–8 (128 pages A7) @ £1.99

□ copy/copies of "Of course I Love You"
ISBN 1–871964–01–6 (96 pages A6) @ £1.99

□ copy/copies of "The Idiots Handbook of Love & Sex"
ISBN 1–871964–08–3 (128 pages A7 size) @ £1.99

□ copy/copies of "The Beginners Guide to Kissing"
ISBN 1–871964–02–4 (64 pages A5) @ £2.50

□ copy/copies of "Tips for a Successful Marriage"
ISBN 1–871964–03–2 (64 pages A5) @ £2.50

□ copy/copies of "The Joy of Fatherhood"
ISBN 1–871964–04–0 (64 pages A5) @ £2.50

□ copy/copies of "Office Hanky Panky"
ISBN 1–871964–05–9 (64 pages A5) @ £2.50

I have enclosed a cheque/postal order for
£_____ made payable to Ideas Unlimited
(Publishing)

Name: _____

Address: _____

Fill in the coupon and send it with your payment to: Ideas
Unlimited (Publishing) PO Box 125, Portsmouth PO1 4PP